MOUNT RUSHMORE

BY BARBARA M. LINDE

Gareth Stevens
PUBLISHING

Please visit our website, www.garethstevens.com. For a free color catalog of all our high-quality books, call toll free 1-800-542-2595 or fax 1-877-542-2596.

Cataloging-in-Publication Data

Names: Linde, Barbara M.
Title: Mount Rushmore / Barbara M. Linde.
Description: New York : Gareth Stevens Publishing, 2019. | Series: Symbols of America | Includes glossary and index.
Identifiers: ISBN 9781538232262 (pbk.) | ISBN 9781538228982 (library bound) | ISBN 9781538232279 (6 pack)
Subjects: LCSH: Mount Rushmore National Memorial (S.D.)–Juvenile literature. | Keystone (S.D.)–Buildings, structures, etc.–Juvenile literature. | Presidents–United States–Monuments–Juvenile literature.
Classification: LCC F657.R8 L523 2019 | DDC 363.6′80973–dc23

Published in 2019 by
Gareth Stevens Publishing
111 East 14th Street, Suite 349
New York, NY 10003

Designer: Sarah Liddell
Editor: Joshua Turner

Photo credits: Cover, p. 1 Lynn Keen/Shutterstock.com; pp. 5, 7 (main) Wollertz/Shutterstock.com; p. 7 (map) Huebi~commonswiki/Wikimedia Commons; p. 9 photo courtesy of Library of Congress; p. 11 critterbiz/Shutterstock.com; p. 13 (Washington and Jefferson) Scewing/Wikimedia Commons; p. 13 (Roosevelt and Lincoln) Stock Montage/Contributor/Archive Photos/Getty Images; p. 15 Everett Historical/Shutterstock.com; p. 17 Joseph Sohm/Shutterstock.com; p. 19 Bettman/Contributor/Bettman/Getty Images; p. 21 gary yim/Shutterstock.com.

Printed in the United States of America

CPSIA compliance information: Batch #CW19GS: For further information contact Gareth Stevens, New York, New York at 1-800-542-2595.

CONTENTS

What Is Mount Rushmore? 4

Where Is Mount Rushmore? 6

The Creator 8

Presidents on the Mountain 10

How Was Mount Rushmore Made? 14

It's Big! 16

Repairs 18

Visiting Mount Rushmore 20

Glossary 22

For More Information 23

Index 24

Boldface words appear in the glossary.

What Is Mount Rushmore?

Mount Rushmore is a huge stone mountain. The faces of four very special presidents are **carved** into the mountain. It's a **symbol** of the United States. It reminds us of how well those presidents led our country.

Where Is Mount Rushmore?

Mount Rushmore is in the state of South Dakota. That is in the midwestern part of the United States. The mountain is part of a **range** called the Black Hills. Mount Rushmore is 5,725 feet high. That's just over 1 mile (1.6 km)! It's named for Charles Rushmore, who visited the area in 1885.

WA

MT

ND

MN

OR

ID

WY

SD

WI

MI

NY

VT NH

ME

MA

RI

CT

MOUNT
RUSHMORE

NE

IA

PA

NV

UT

IL

IN

OH

NJ

DE

CA

CO

KS

MO

KY

WV

VA

MD

AZ

NM

OK

AR

TN

NC

MS

AL

GA

SC

TX

LA

AK

HI

FL

BLACK HILLS

The Creator

Doane Robinson wanted people to visit South Dakota. He thought a huge stone **sculpture** would interest them. Gutzon Borglum was a **sculptor** and **patriot**. He chose the place and planned the sculpture. When he died, his son, Lincoln, finished the project.

Presidents on the Mountain

Four of our nation's greatest presidents are on Mount Rushmore. George Washington was the leader of the army in the Revolutionary War. Thomas Jefferson was the third president. He bought a piece of land that made the country twice as big.

Theodore Roosevelt helped workers improve their rights and get better jobs. He created the first national parks. Abraham Lincoln was president during the Civil War. He helped end the war and free the slaves. He brought the country back together after the war.

DATES OF PRESIDENCY

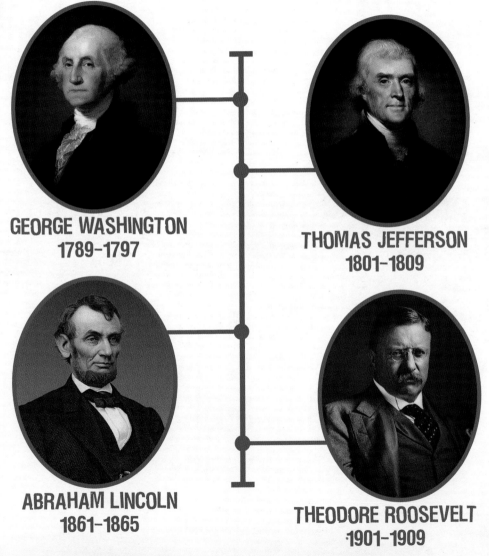

GEORGE WASHINGTON
1789–1797

THOMAS JEFFERSON
1801–1809

ABRAHAM LINCOLN
1861–1865

THEODORE ROOSEVELT
1901–1909

How Was Mount Rushmore Made?

First, workers blasted away some of the stone. Then, others hung from the side of the mountain in special chairs. They used tools to shape the faces. Every day, the workers walked up and down 700 steps! The work began in 1927 and ended in 1941.

It's Big!

Mount Rushmore is the largest sculpture in the world. Each head is the same size as three adult giraffes! See how each part of the face compares to the size of many different animals on the next page.

PART OF THE SCULPTURE	SIZE	ANIMAL SIZE
HEAD	60 FEET (18 M) HIGH	THREE GIRAFFES
EACH EYE	11 FEET (3 M) WIDE	AN ALLIGATOR
MOUTH	18 FEET (5.5 M) LONG	A PYTHON
NOSE	21 FEET (6 M) LONG	A KILLER WHALE

Repairs

The heat, cold, wind, rain, and snow cause cracks in the sculpture. Workers seal the cracks with a waterproof material called caulk. Machines on the mountain tell the temperature and sense movements every day. Workers can fix problems right away.

Visiting Mount Rushmore

More than 2 million people visit each year. You can't climb the mountain, but you can see the faces from the ground. Movies and museums tell its history. Take a tour online if you can't get there in person!

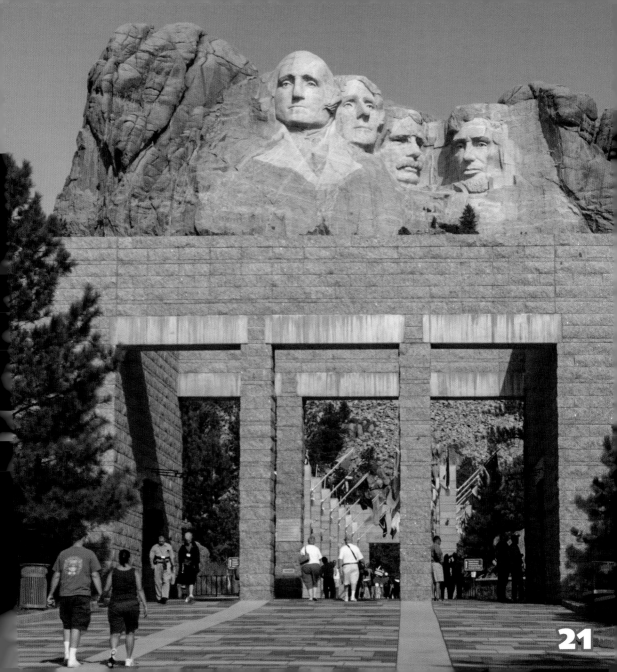

GLOSSARY

carved: formed by cutting and shaping a material such as stone

patriot: a person who loves their country

range: a line or row of mountains

sculptor: an artist who creates shapes with stone, wood, metal, or other matter

sculpture: a shape created with stone, wood, metal, or other matter

symbol: a picture, object, or shape that stands for something else

FOR MORE INFORMATION

BOOKS

Gunderson, Jessica. *Mount Rushmore*. North Mankato, MN: Capstone Press, 2014.

Jango-Cohen, Judith. *Mount Rushmore*. Minneapolis, MN: Lerner Publications, 2013.

WEBSITES

Fun Mount Rushmore Facts for Kids
www.sciencekids.co.nz/sciencefacts/engineering/mountrushmore.html
Find out STEM (Science, Technology, Engineering, Mathematics) facts about building Mount Rushmore.

Mount Rushmore
www.nps.gov/moru/index.htm
Learn about the history and current events at Mount Rushmore National Park.

INDEX

Black Hills 6

Borglum, Gutzon 8

Borglum, Lincoln 8

caulk 18

Civil War 12

Jefferson, Thomas 10

Lincoln, Abraham 12

Revolutionary War 10

Robinson, Doane 8

Roosevelt, Theodore 12

Rushmore, Charles 6

sculptor 8

sculpture 8, 16, 18

South Dakota 6, 8

Washington, George 10